The Calculus of Imaginaries

Also by Gerard Grealish

Anthology

Palpable Clock: 25 Years of Mulberry Poets
(coedited with Karen Blomain, Nancy Deisroth, and David Elliott)

The Calculus of Imaginaries

Poems by
Gerard Grealish

NY Books™

The New York Quarterly Foundation, Inc.
Beacon, New York

NYQ Books™ is an imprint of The New York Quarterly Foundation, Inc.

The New York Quarterly Foundation, Inc.
P. O. Box 470
Beacon, NY 12508

www.nyq.org

Second Edition

The First Edition of this book was publsihed by Nightshade Press.

Set in New Baskerville

Layout and Design by Raymond P. Hammond

Cover Photograph by Susan Luckstone Jaffer

Author Photo by Trudy Gerlach

Library of Congress Control Number: 2020938818

ISBN: 978-1-63045-076-2

for my sons

Jareth and Beckett

in the calculus of love

Contents

III. The Transfer Principle

IV. Impossible Conditions

calculus of imaginaries: a method of investigating the nature of imaginary quantities required to fulfill apparently impossible conditions, using $\sqrt{-1}$ (the square root of negative one) as a unit.

Webster's New Twentieth Century Dictionary
Second Edition, Copyright 1979 by Simon & Schuster

I

Imaginary Roots

Eyes

The dogs are barking.
I see them stretching their chains
in a straight line noses
sighting eyes to some point
in the fields. I see nothing
but they bark
                they strain
against the trees till the bark
chips off to the ground. Five minutes
of this and raised lips
close on teeth eyes
lose focus the links grow slack
and they turn toward their
houses and the shade.

Ribs cave
beneath fur the wood grunts
as they collapse
and in one gesture
                        rest
their jaws on their front
paws—
a rush of breath
                and dust flies
one inch before them
settles just outside.

In the fields the wind
bends pale grasses and releases them.

Vector

It is morning and a woman's
distance can be determined
through the pores
                of a screen as she moves
down
an empty sidewalk; a face
pushes its nose
against mesh
            so the eyes can see
more
      as her back
becomes her body
becomes a black
speck turning a corner.

A boy remembers
yelling
          her name her turning
to wave
even after there is nothing
but a concrete line
              thinning the further
it points away.

Void

of body of voice—
man who never moved
outside my mother's lips
calling you
so mournfully
father I could feel you
in her breath.

   *   *   *

The breeze
the blurred trees
the leaves long since fallen
and crushed into sediment—
testament to the mind
once behind your furrowed brow
the stare beneath receding slicked-back hair
leaving little to realize little to spare

                              as if you knew *Pater*

only eyes could speak
in this photograph
and this look would have to last.

   *   *   *

From the bowels of being
an oeuvre for whom only one
mover exists I insist
you rise up
           bare your bald head
and tell me:

What shit is this that floats
in your image what refuge
in being your son?

Tell me
about that hour you bored me
into her
            both of you
gasping
            your sweat
trickling
from skin to skin.

Genesis

Imagine fire
wavering before us
                    shadows
extending to the dark

before Gaelic before Sanskrit,
when meanings were
finely tuned on the human string.

Our fingers grope
for the Braille of ourselves; hands
travel the contours
of consciousness reading neck
and collarbone
                    breast and rib
pelvic perimeter within which
we are centered

our vessel rocking
on the amniotic sea our wanting
nothing more than the current
taking us.

An Evening with Guinness

The crunch of gravel beneath our feet. Too dark
to see in our faces what
makes us blood. Walking to the pub
my cousin John and I
find our way quietly.

Earlier the gray open
sky above us we had walked
this lane between these thatched
cottages this flat rocky land the same
Martin knew the same fathers
before him—Paddy remembered for his strength
scything the fields Michael of whom
nothing is known
but his name.

This is the Galway Martin left.
Though in America he died
before his son's birth though his son fathered me

                                        and died
in my infancy
after one hundred years
I am here.

John lives in my grandfather's house. His wife
puts three potatoes on my plate and I help
herd ten cows from the pasture back
to the barn.

The lineage faint I ask:
Who will be the shanachies?
and I see in the shaking of his head
John fears as I do our sons
may not feel the need.

Now Guinness
waits for us and Duffy behind the bar
to serve the pints.

El Niño 1997

No se puede vivir sin amar were the words on the house
—Malcolm Lowry, *Under the Volcano*

Out of the almost endlessly parched
earth of northern Chile
                              yellows
reds
blues.

Wildflowers not seen for decades
arise. *Arriba!* in the Atacama.
Sin flores no se puede amar.
Sin amor no se puede vivir.

A homeless man must be
drunk again. *No es posible* he mutters and
as if he were right
                    reports
of rodents rampaging of rat crap floating in zephyrs
resonate over the air waves
as if the lungs of local residents
were screaming mantras were shrieking *"Hanta!*

Hanta! Hanta! Hantavirus
you are killing us" *Sin muerte*
no se puede vivir. In Acapulco
the little children haunt the streets
out of thirst. *Agua*
                    agua por favor.
Sin agua no se puede vivir.

El niño strange child
your warm breath dries up the riviera

dampens the desert
                         drops snow
where snow seldom falls and drought
where metal rusts as a matter of course.

Then there are flowers.

Whose child are you anyway?
I can almost hear you
crying out *"No sé! No sé!"*
Oh so beautifully.

Monologue in Scranton's Historic Ironworks

Where men sweated and heat
smelted iron
                    icicles
hang from stone; pigeons
flap against cylindrical walls
leave droppings
on the stone floor.

Hard to tear down
this brick upon brick
built thick as prison walls
and no need to. Nothing
wants to be here. Out of sight
the city prospers
cut from the same rock ridge.

Here a shouting voice
grows further away
as if it spoke in another time.

The Fraction

Above the surface
the one who immersed you in breath
thick with whiskey smiled
as he threw you into air.

Among the denominators yours
left a legacy of free fall figures
of yourself in the abstract holding on
to nothing you could imagine—
music endlessly inside
your head
              outside water
that could drown you.

Swim! the bastard commands
now no more than an arm stroke away
waiting in deeper water.

Kill! he dares
as you with his last name
throw yourself at his ghost.

Inertia

Nodding off again
to a thought that might be
worth staying awake for—

if only I weren't
so tired if only the wordless
nature of it
were not already
dissolving

into silhouettes
flying away from a tree's
branches the remnants of
dusk of songs of wings
                    flapping

A View of Scranton

From the Hill
                    Southside at dusk. Houses
with the merest spaces between them seem joined
to house the quiet outside. Stones
in cemeteries seem a continuum of stone;
there are certain mausoleums
not unlike the steeples and mosques scattered here.

Here there is a power the builders could not divine
as if the place itself conspired a finishing touch.
The clatter of forks and knives goes unheard
and to the west the sky that is orange darkens.

Trumpet

Between trembling lips
the first phonetics of apnea and schwa
the *wah-wah* of the inarticulate
duende Miles knew—
beauty born from loss
its dance
its bed.

Hear now
in the vaguely remembered cries how
we listen
to death the constant
swish and swash

of the amniotic sea we cannot escape
unless we wail.

II

Infinitesimals

Squeak

A violinist
          her jaw fused
with a Stradivarius her wrist
bending in trigonometric
function
          carves
out of strings a scream
like last evening's

that awakened me
from a book.

The snap of the trap the simultaneous
shriek took me to
the memory of quivering
jowls bristling whiskers.

Somewhere between the small world
of living and the large one of death
is the dying. The squeak of it
is the violinist blurring her bow
like Valkyrie wings.

Two Gifts

Yesterday the dog
brought back a woodchuck. The flies
were busy on the dark brown fur. They scattered
when I slid the shovel
underneath. The bloated belly
rolled easily the teeth smiled yellow even through
the first dirt that fell
in its grave. Its ears
were small and perked
its head bent toward its feet
as though listening.

Today the fields
came back with the dog. He had been
rolling in cow dung again. He
loves it and a bitch in heat
down the road. He
cowered when I told him
to get the hell away from me
just like yesterday
when he put his death-smell jaws around
my forearm. It will be a week
before he smells like a dog.

Four Oranges

I *Florida*

Every Christmas—oranges—
a bushel from the aunt
who lived in Florida.

When the birds moved in flocks
my mother said they were flying
to Florida. I asked
when the birds seemed a black cloud

of gnats in the distance *Is that
Florida where the birds are now?* and she
would answer *No
it is further than you can see
than even the birds*

can see. And I would remember that
when I bit
into an orange.

II *Friends*

We would sit
behind the local store
eating popsicles
in the summer heat.

We would lick
the ice melting
toward our fingers
and when we had cleaned the ice off
flick

popsicle sticks
into a pile on the ground.

Like clowns
we would stick our
tongues out—

grape and orange.

III Tea Time

Mornings
sitting at the table
over cups
of orange pekoe tea.

Sipping
in the quiet.

The mist
rising slowly
uncovering
the mountain.

IV Stasis

I return
after the October rains
to the redwood
table under the pines.

The brisk wind
against my face
the emptiness
of the place

give being there
a sense
of what has hardly moved—
the trees

the grill's
orange rust
and my arms on the table.

The Art of Flying

Wild turkeys peck at gravel
in the driveway; slim pickings
must have brought them down
from the uphill woods so steep
they couldn't stop running
till they got here.

Transfixed at dusk
I am the silhouette they see
framed in the front window
like the shadow
of a tree.

I see nothing
but their long necks dipping
to the ground their long
sticklike legs their
iridescent feathers from which
their wings rise.

I watch till the light fades
and they begin their slow ascent
back to the high woods—

their walking a form

of casting shadows
on the full moon.

Africam.com

A lot of screeching and squawking...as if
some predator unheard from yet
advances
            as if some low-lying branch
stretched almost to the snapping point
will whip into bloody pulp
whoever's in its wake.

The intermittent silence
does not pause the continuing
what if...what if
as if contingency unrealized
were the real horror.

What happens next
is hard to say. *What if*
whatever it is were to turn its head
its instinct distracted by
some sound
            some scent
                        some movement
more compelling
that beckons it elsewhere?

What if—mouse in hand
witness to the waterhole at Nkorho Pan
the ripple-free placidity
of its water—

god-that-I-am
hears the phone ring?

Whetstone

Ice is part of it.
Under snow ground to slush
by wheels spinning and spinning is that

smoothness made smoother
than skin
            touching skin in the sweat

of August. The curves
of our spines
            angle us

make circles
in this small space again and again
as though we were

slipping on ice
ice were
melting in the grind.

Pointing

Clear cold night
above us the gestalt of Orion
                        Canis Major
constellations I cannot name
as I walk the dog down
the hard dirt of Gritman Road
to the highway.

The leash now taut
he leans toward the other
side the distant engine
of a Mack truck humming
its horsepower to sleep.

There is something across the way
my dog wants—the dog he saw
and whose bark he heard
yesterday in the light or maybe the great
horned owl that hooted
gruffly and invisibly
last night from a tree over there
where the Edward Hopper-looking house
sits and where the moon
sometimes shines.

You're not going! I admonish him
knowing there's death
in the spaces between risk
and desire.

Point! I command
and he does so
perfectly poised
for what otherwise
might be his.

37

Alms

After "Misery' (a photograph) by Carole Lins

Pedestrians pass her
as if she were a fixture no more
animate than a metallic barricade
dividing sidewalk
from excavation
                a foot from the deep
pit that might swallow them—
                        a great risk
not worth considering.

Look at her body.
The hunchbacked curve of spine
under an oversized coat belies
straight legs within the peasant dress
but for the plumb line fall
of fabric from the small of her back
to concrete.

How perfectly straight
the walking cane
upon which she rests
her left hand then her right
the paper cup
dangling from her fingers.

The Clock

Light flickers in the stream's bed
softly
        light that further downstream
grows on the water blinding.

This light in the tunnel by the tracks
glints from rock midway in darkness.

Certain days we crouch near the edge. The stillness
of small fish balancing near the pond's surface
is limitless: their eyes never blink their bodies
angled in a random cluster are minutes that do not turn
in the green water in the afternoon light.

The Work

Each year the snap
of brittle wood; old locusts.
I'm dragging
              broken branches
from the road again; someone
must clear the way.

The old trees
lose more limbs now in a year
than they can grow. From ice and wind
next winter's fire.

III

The Transfer Principle

The Twinge

To say I love you is not to say
all things are forgotten. Sometimes
dreaming at night beside you
I lose track. The bed
could be any bed.

The phone rings.
Hello I answer. *Hello*
I repeat before the click.

It is not over. In a quiet room
far removed someone
thinks of you
and in another
someone thinks of me.

The Glass Eye

After "J. L.'s Eye" (paper & graphite) by Diana Perciballi

I.

It took you by surprise;
no matter what you said or how
you looked you were caught
in a lie its unwavering
stare out of nowhere a conscience
precariously unbalanced
between the brown
iris and the pupil's
black abyss.

II.

One night it took her
to what she thought she missed:
her own bed with him
looking down at her
blindsided by the only eye
she could see in the bedroom's dark
taking her in
          all of her
in to the moonlight that speck
of white reflected.

III.

We took it to mean
nothing in its concentric
view could be ruled out not even
the violence of rending
piece by piece the flesh it
desired and pierced
with an intimation of love.

Nothing was beneath it.
Nothing above.

IV.

It was a god's eye;
its crystalline vision
again and again turned
on itself invisible
to all of us the way we are
to ourselves the way
we say a word
and it goes silent.

Marathon

for Beckett

Though you have just run half
of what will be before you three weeks from now
you are still on this long distance
call catching your breath wanting
nothing more you say
than the balance that brings to breath
a certain peace.

I can only imagine
the rhythm of your breathing like mine
when I ran so many miles less so many
years ago and a crow spooked
by the sight of me and the small thunder
of my feet cawed its way out

of a tree
and the blackness of itself
into the dawn.

The Migration

Geese fly south so high up you must
point them out—
black specks near the edge
of a cloud.

We watch
even after the sky
bears nothing
but itself—as though
we remember clearly what it is
to forget

Escarpment Trail

for Brenna

Had I not forgotten exactly
what it meant we would have
hiked a different course back the same
we took to North Lookout where
we'd seen hawk and vulture
glide in the easterly winds off
Ridge Overlook and the River of Rocks.

But the city inside me paled
against her seven-year-old insistence:
*Don't you want to know
what an "escarpment" is?*

Were she not so stubborn
neither of us would be
clambering over these endless
boulders
        crevices sloping
toward the abyss the red paint
splotches marking a rocky trail
like blood.

Halfway back she pauses.
The distance from one rock
to another outreaches her arm. She's
scared as I hold out
the hand she grabs

stronger and surer
than a moment later when I
fall an old man
she cannot lift the one her father put
his trust in for whom
she hopes love has powers
beyond itself.

Three Heads

I.

His paws
imprint the white that has fallen
so far in the night.

Cerberus sniffs the yellowish
green scent of himself
on a snowbank.

II.

The crescent moon is rocking.

In the biting cold the hemlock's
creaking is the voice
of a ghost ship the old wood
stretched to the snapping point.

Cerberus hears
the next wind
coming.

III.

At the end of the road
Ursa Major and Orion's Belt above
Cerberus points
to a meteorite streaking.

Bounce

Three mornings he sits
on a bench in the courthouse square
rubber ball bouncing
from concrete to his hand
mustache flashing
above pursed lips.

Pock. Pock. Pock.
The small sphere strikes this large one.
In shorts sneakers and a baseball cap
belly bulging below the T-shirt
he never speaks
and never misses.

What love we ask
could he ever have? And later
we gasp for breath and want no more
than his power to look again and again
at what comes back
and to hold it.

The Calling

for Maggie and Tanoy

It's clear from the photograph
something is
sacred between you

as if snow and cold
conspired to create warmth
in the holding

of each other's hand
as if out of silence
faint rhythms

became the percussion
of your feet
your presence

the mantra
of your breathing
deepening

step by step
the winds within you
whispering

like the air itself.

Ice
on the running trail
cannot deter you.

You fill
the emptiness
when it needs

to be filled.
It calls you.

Boaz

And it came to pass at midnight that the man was afraid and turned himself: and behold a woman lay at his feet.
—Ruth 3:8

Boaz was not a young man
and about him little is known before
Ruth came into the threshing floor washed
anointed to lie at his feet. A stranger
to the Ephrathite she could not fathom
the love that brought her from Moab
clinging to Naomi; and he could not
rest from the moment she woke him.

Alone so long without reprieve
he had forgotten a life
no longer his
wanted as the flesh is
before it's been had and after again
in the numberless days of plowing
sowing
        reaping
                and threshing.
Yet once
there was a woman…

And the fields were still there the rows
of barley—after harvest
an emptiness to be reworked
against drought and pestilence
fear at midnight
that nothing would come of it again
much less the old love he felt turning himself
as Ruth removed his shoes.

The Cry

for Jareth

"I'll be back." —Arnold Schwarzenegger, *The Terminator*

I'm back now

even as his skin melts even as metal
drips off his empty core
and he drags himself
                              with one arm
toward Sarah
pregnant with the future
he hopes to annihilate.

In a recoil of flames
the specter
of John Connor no more
than the celluloid of Sarah's
photo burning
love to its negative…

In this dark theater you are
mesmerized. In the movie's
flickering light your face
is taut as it must have been
fifteen years before when
contraction by contraction
your mother felt you
announcing yourself—you
who had had enough of incessant
amniotic baptisms.

I never heard your first
cry though I imagine it
something like mine when I first

learned of you—an unspeakable
disbelief that anything like you could be
born of me: a wailing
                    more resonant
than words.

Tone

for Tony Marino

The crown of your head
whirls in monastic prayer
as you and the wood you embrace
become an utterance
                          your neck
round and round fusing
with the neck of your bass
                              your arms
holding its body close.

For love and loss
you stroke you pluck you bow.
You will not let us
forget the strings the stories
you have learned by heart and leave
wordless for us to fill
with language.

How you shake your head No
telling us *Don't forget* how
the shaking of your head takes
back and forth and turns
its cycles into circles

is a revolution
of blood traveling down
to your fingers a groping for
the memory that might be.

IV

Impossible Conditions

Somewhere Else

Caviar and chateaubriand
embellish our tables; we drink
Chateauneuf-du-Pape down to the dregs
and later doze before TV
                                    flies
at the eyes of children
                                    their protruding
bellies belied by bones
bulging almost bursting through skin—

all in the "Third World." Not here
the famine in Sudan
the war in Sri Lanka. Not here
the Ebola in the Congo
                                    nor the earthquakes
in Haiti and Nicaragua.

We keep
counting sheep where no sheep graze
until half-crazed we awake
to AIDS spreading
                                    the world over the first plane
crashing into the North Tower the second
into the South.

And with one click
of the remote the blinking screen
shutters like an eyelid to a close
the countless waves
of consciousness
                                    unconsciousness
lapping our minds with whispers
magical thinking and
Maginot lines.

Possessed

How can she leave
the horses
when the one who tends them once tended
her
        and she knows them
each by name
                    even
the lame one that should be
put down
                the mare
with markings only a breeder
could divine?

In his wildest
imaginings no horse
with such proportions such
eyes and such
a mane could be other than
mythology. And so he grooms her
along with the others whom he can't
bear to see without her
whom he can't
bear her to be without.

There is no race to be won
                            no show
to be had other than this
gathering of beasts
with no burden other than his
to bear: the grooming the feeding
the setting out to pasture the herding
of them back to the stables
when dusk comes.

This is his life now
which he can't bear to be without
which she can't bear
for another day till that day
comes and she sees him
who spent the night stabled beside her
ambling in first light

toward the barn
where the myth is intact.

The Entrée

Who would have wanted it
this way? You don't;
you cringe at his calling you
wife and wanting
                so he says
no more than you at the table
                        food
now a medium for what cannot be
served no matter the seasoning—herbs
grown for years in the garden
                        dried
on stems
            crushed into flecks
garnishing the main course
                        the sterile
dinnerware.

You are not hungry you say;
you excuse yourself for time
in the kitchen with pots and pans
a mind racing with glimpses
of his skeleton. It is the way
he picks at his food as though searching for fuel
in a culm dump the way he will say
with half his plate untouched
                      how good
it was how good to be together
that leaves a lump in your throat—nothing
compared to later when he will stand before you
for a hug a goodnight kiss a certain
listlessness in the dark.

Disrepair

Repair this house? What tools
after so many years could
mend this warped wood meant
to house what it cannot?

Warmth leaves
through its crevices. Cold
creeps in. Under the down nothing
flies as it used to. Wind
whines what is no longer.

The tools are in the shed
as they have been for years
                              rotting
in the damp dark corners of wood
so warped it can hardly house itself
much less what love would take
to repair.

In the air there is no mind
other than the one no one has
to think us. It almost
dries things out
                      cloning itself
in a rustle of sheets as we
barely listening
fall asleep to the rain.

No Trespassing

We have tried to keep things private. Stashed away
the boxes in attics and cellars collect dust the journals
stuck behind beneath or between other books
                                    in drawers
among clothes letters trinkets
                        God knows what
contain the self that became another self.

We have tried to keep
the memory quiet. Better
to forget we say better to make believe
it belongs to someone else.

But how can we keep each other out? How can we
cart all these things each day up and down the stairs
before dawn or after midnight while the other sleeps
and out the back door? How can we burn them in the yard
so that the fire is not too bright
                                    throw them out
so strays do not scatter them all about? How can we
when there is so much not meet each other embarrassed
that a stranger who won't be loved takes us
to a place in the dark?

The Stranger

She told me she made a fire.
I imagine the gifts
sacrificial—the stuffed walrus
squatting in flames its eyes
dumb and docile even as the plastic
drips down.

The silver pendants—
Durga
      Shakti
in metal too metal to melt—
clink through the grates.

And more. Photographs
of her and me smiling
                    at some distance
arms around the kids—burning
back to negatives
and beyond.

Now she said
everything before those ashes
is dead. Whoever comes
will be someone else.

The Step Falls

There is a desire to dive into this wall
of water
            drench our bodies in the rush of white and plunge
into the pool below.

It is not a sane desire. Though it is cool there
and here the heat wears away at us
                              steps
of stone brick are bedrock to the falls.

Thirty feet across and forty down it is a power
we would be taken by. After months
waiting to bare our bodies to this sun we wait now
for the tingling movement of the falls.
We see the vague outlines of stone
that seem the design of water.

Grand Jeté

for Suze

In the darkness your face hovers
above the dashboard's digital glow.

On the radio the sitar
the tabla the mournful
voice of the singer
extract love
from pain as you drive down
this back road again this corridor
between trees.

It is almost a dance
of nirvana when the doe springs
into air in no time out of nowhere—
but then the thumping sounds
of metal striking bone of grace turned
to chaos the bouncing on pavement
the collapsing into a clump.

In the beam
of your headlights the deer its eyes
                              confused
lifts its head and looks too late
at what has arrived.

The Kitchen

Though I am pictured as well holding you
with the dog in your arms
                                    such happiness
seldom seen was yours in this photograph—
your eyes closed your smile and body
caved in to this moment
where whiskey on the counter
                                    a light
above the sink and an open cabinet door give way
to night outside the windows. Love perhaps

but seen from this distance nothing
on the face of things is anything
clear. Warm as the dog
warm as the whiskey in our bloodstreams
you might have felt this
is where it all comes together
as if even the inanimate had conspired to
create what you wanted.

I cannot say
what I wanted. Home perhaps
where captured as they are things happen
seem certain

as in this photograph
where you are pictured happy and where
my eyes are closed too.

Penance

Papers upon papers upon papers—
old bills to remind me what I owed
twenty years ago tax returns
well past the threat of audit
clippings
of news so old their yellow tint
forebodes how they will break
like bay leaves in my fingers

and more: old magazines and books
I meant to read but never did
others I've read and hardly remember—
characters and plots in settings
I once imagined mine. I've kept tickets
from planes buses and trains
theaters where I traveled
out of the body.

Memorialized here are licenses
long expired records
of health and the lack of it
births and deaths.

Forgive me now
for wanting an end
to all these things you generated
by having me for envisioning
with pleasure a garbage truck's jaws
crushing these traces
of who I have been
that includes you
your letters your photos.

Isn't it enough
that you are in my face
that I am in my children's
and that when morning comes
I will stare out the window
and see what might have been?

Maxima Culpa

for Andrzej Nadolny

You kneel down
like an acolyte on the southbound
train's floor an altar now
elevated by sacrifice a man
turning blue
                    gasping before you
touch his wrist
                    find the risk
of your mouth on his
infinitesimal.

You do not ask
how among so many passengers so densely packed
he fell
          or how he spread himself
out full length on his back
without touching a shoe. So many shoes
surround him now as if they had all
come of their own accord to worship
this space he now has
apart from them.

You take deep breaths—
breathe and arrest
                    breathe and arrest—
then into his trachea expel them;
from your lungs to his
whatever can live in this air will
and will not otherwise as now you must
compress his chest *rest and compress*
rest and compress.

Now the fist that once pounded
your altar boy's breast for forgiveness

71

pounds open-handed his heart.
You want to hear it.
The beating
is only your own.

And the words you once spoke before a priest
return in English as if they were
untranslatable
              as if they were the Latin
your father once spoke kneeling
before you knew him:

Mea culpa
              mea culpa
mea maxima culpa.

V

_____

Transcendent Curves

The Recall

Something about a loose link
and loss of steering
I had heard on the radio

but the huge curve
was already upon me—
the trees the deep

ravine turning
over and over in my headlights
as I turned the wheel.

After in some still dark I imagined
how mangled the car must be how
my face must be a mask

of pulp and blood that would
scare you if you saw me
calling your name.

What if it were you when
the road started winding
and the tires could not

hold? Would you
call for me
or are we simply

speechless at the end
not by design
but by love recalled?

Saguaros

I

Limbs
75
    100 years
in the making reach up
like the calcified arms
of Hindu fakirs worshipping
                      Muslim
fakirs begging in the crowded streets
of Calcutta.

Time
will lop them off
though 40
        even 50 feet
tall—the pedestrian foot
of themselves squashing themselves
much like the white
waxy flowers of May open
one evening
        close
the next
        never
to reopen only to
ripen to green
fruits that burst with red
pulp
      the ferment
of which is wine
and stupor.

II

Sanctus Sanctus Sanctus
or not—what does it
matter beyond some elaborate
function whose value depends
on functions
or doesn't? Saguaros
have withstood the mushrooms

                the fallout

of atoms divided

           the chain
of energy released
by him who says I think
therefore. Better
not to think; better therefore to drink
rain as the cacti do.

Om Om Om
Which came first
the rain or the ritual? What world
will be ruined if one
is not
a function of the other?

III

What world?
As peyote exploded in colors
what world was ruined when
Mescaleros crouching in sand chewed themselves
into the spiritual?

There is no world
other than this where Saguaros at dusk are
silhouettes slipping from light
into night's black lining.

The Falcon Club
for Jareth

I imagine your small fist
striking the pillow the fluffed-up
effigy flattened by one blow
after another.

Give it to me.
Let me have it.

Was it Italy
where the ceiling fan whirled
the dark into a blur an arc
of insomnia spinning
even into the light? *Too late*
to go back I reasoned then the premise
of unresolved arguments in the kitchen
long lost to cigarette smoke
                              my fist
pounding their points into the table
my rages unable
to sustain themselves above your mother's
answers
            the clatter of porcelain
and silver at the sink.

I imagine your eyes
open
        my diatribes oblivious
to your dreams of flying
                              the both of us
in the pandemonium
denying what exists
                        waiting

for the Falcon's next
edition to save us.

Love is just
another criminal enterprise. Uncertain
the Falcon rises now above the metropolis
his anger at the monstrous
shadows below a source
of his intent his furious descent
into himself.

Now comes the victim
and the vanquished hardly distinguishable

                                        the victor

as incomprehensible to himself
as he was to begin with. A heart
as if illustrated in these pages
beats out of itself
a pair of wings.

Your small fingers once
gripped my forearm like talons.

Look.
Here you are in midair an infant
in a floppy white hat floating above
my fingers. This photo
captures your laugh
your faith in flying.

Laughing too I appear
crazed with certainty.

The Hug

for Beckett

As though I were about to leave
but never would go
                      never really go
I feel your arms almost in disbelief
wrapped around me your strong hands
pulling the cumbersome weight
of my torso against yours my heart
the palpable clock of being
your father turned back
twenty-five years.

Intangible fears survive
in your embrace; your hands
grip the shirt on my back
as mine grab yours
                    the little shake the almost
indiscernible aftershock
of what brought us here: marriage
and divorce the brute force
of the mind mending
the heart's losses.

I remember only now
the quiet latching of the door lock the cold
air that November day catching my breath
                                    dispersing it
in clouds no sooner visible than not
the bare trees
branching out the gray sky
endless.

In the stillness
of so many days since
your five-year-old eyes question

promises swirling in the blood the confluence
of your mother's and mine the undivined
force of the flow.

What is there to know
of my going? Undefined still
are the drunken and maniacal
rantings after midnight in rented rooms their walls
the stage of shadows
                          suicidal
in the morning light.

What right
did I have to leave—
the years of your small palm in my grasp
an anguish I will never see the last of.
What right now to return?
The questions burn your diminutive
footprints in the snow melted long ago
dissolved like mine
and impossible to track.

What right
do I have other than love
to assert—which cannot think
clearly of itself and which
                          instinctively
comes as I do now
to feel yours.

Hold tight my son.

Wavelengths

for the Coastal Research & Education Society of Long Island and
for the Sea Shepherd Conservation Society

Geyser!
in the Great South Channel signals
an exhalation beneath
                    a fathomless
beast we have come to
witness

as if its massiveness
might tell us
of infinity the in-
finitesimal

as if it were we who were
stranded on the beaches
of Isla San José Lanzarote
and Fuerteventura succumbing
to the sonar
boomeranged below.

*   *   *

The waters
of the Bay of Biscay of Nantucket
and Montauk washed
the blood that we let
and in Sag Harbor the rusted
harpoons the sun-bleached jawbones
make a museum of massacre.

Yet the humpback
flashes its fluke
a black & white
that could only be "Pisces"

83

migrating from Maine's
Gulf her calf
in synchronized rhythm.

Neither needs us
but neither are oblivious as they surface
for deep breaths
in the seascape
                    their eyes

upon us—like those
of "Flyingfish" rising starboard
in the fountains of his force
crashing crashing

his fifty-foot thirty-ton
bulk
        rocketing
from the depths

to which he thunderously
returns.

*   *   *

Even now whaling ships
patrol glacier coasts
for cetacean mist.

Mothers and calves rise
whalers aim
harpoon cannons at shadows
wavering in sun.

Black
as the fin whale surfacing in its own
blood a vessel
                parts the red
waters of Antarctica.

Amid icebergs
whales and floating factories
the bosun calls out
Captain
are we ready?

and he hears
above the slapping waves
Yes.

Ram! Keep ramming
till they stop!

*   *   *

It's early morning.
On the close misty horizon
they surround the boat
barely visible their backs
curving on the surface flawlessly
the continuum of
                emerging
returning.

Grab hold
we tell ourselves *Grab*
hold!

Carpenter/Poet at the Gate

for Michael Macklin, Poetry Editor

I imagine you inviting strangers
into the fold
               finding in the cut
of their words a grain that draws you
in
    knots burned
from branches born of the mother trunk.

Beyond saw
             axe and chisel
hammer and nail
                  I imagine you
discovering the wood; beyond the pen
you find the wounds open

and dress them
not with paint but the transparent
stain of yourself.
In the scars will be
the words.

Investigator

for Frank Grippi

Your current investigation
is an internal affair—cancerous
tumors grow in your body
indifferent to you as you
look for clues
to thwart them.

You did it the old way you
used to say no cutting
corners when being there
might disclose a twitch
in a witness's eye a stutter in his
answers. At the silent crime scenes
you'd listen for the victims'
voices
       look within
the empty rooms
for the possible.

Not one to report
meaningless things you'd wait
for a break in the case.

You wait now
in the respite hospice
allows; you will follow
the evidence wherever it goes.

The Afterglow

for Kathy

Her hometown suburb seems out of place. Too quiet
to imagine her here among manicured lawns
block after block of houses and flowers.

A silk blouse and a print
skirt cannot put her here. Neither can
rouge cheeks.

Pallbearer now I think of
the books she read
the music she listened to.
Like Sharon she is a distant galaxy blinking
its image from ten billion years ago
as if for the first time.

On the kitchen wall of her place in the city the chipped
paint that uncovers older paint reminds me
of her at the table. Now
without a word she pours the wine
into my glass into hers. Between us
there is nothing more
than a ruby glow.

Anesthesia

The red hand above you
flicks off seconds fleck
by black fleck; the black hand
twitches interminable minutes in this
sterile room. Soon
the orderlies will come
to wheel me away.

Worry etches itself
into your faces
its inflection in your voices.

The clock's face
mostly white the wall
surgeon green
soon eyes
of a masked team
will peer down
in piercing light.

Time in the OR
will not be mine alone you console
but before long
your words
like the anesthesiologist's
drift off.

The saw buzzes through bone
to the heart of consciousness
darkened.

The Marrow

Slumped in the wheelchair he's somewhere
beyond the waiting room
behind the glasses
draped over his nose his closed
eyes. You can imagine
drool syruping
from the misshapen mouth the parted
lips

but not this
music within his moans
                        this spacing
of mournful tones between
silences—

the loss of her
embedded in his consciousness
whatever there is of it
outside his expressionless face his
body crammed between the metallic
pedals and leathered
back.

The tune
is in his bones. At ninety
he sings to her and you
listen until
there is no you
outside his song.

Saxology

Eyes
lust for the serpent in it
                              ears
allured by its psalms
as if sirens sing through it
of years yet to come
waters yet traversed.

It's the *Out of this World*
Trane played to Elvin's
crashing cymbals;
it's Lieb's *Shape Shifters* dust-storming
among the nomads in Stephans'
arrhythmic beat.

It's Trane's *Naima*
Lieb's *Carissima*
                      Ornette's
Lonely Woman...

the curves of it
the dance of holding it
so close the valves are vertebrae
of the spine you glide
your fingers over.

Prayer

Rib cage out and in—
love is
the old dog breathing on the night
of its death.

Pray with me. Let me
feel your bone your flesh
as if they were not within
another grasp as if
there were not things thought of
that might be asked.

Rotation

Quiet as the vultures
wheeling in the high winds
dark wings still against the light—

clock
of the moment the gliding
                              the invisible
eyes the beautiful tilt

of feathers circling
last breaths below—

an eternity of air

taken in
let go.

Acknowledgments

With thanks to the following publications, in which some of these poems first appeared, sometimes in earlier versions:

1998 Daybook: MPWA (Mulberry Poets & Writers Association): "A View of Scranton"
All Roads Will Lead You Home (virtual artists collective): "Squeak," "Genesis," "Boaz," and "The Calling"
The Bad Henry Review: "The Clock"
The Café Review: "El Niño 1997," "Marathon," "Escarpment Trail," "Carpenter/Poet at the Gate"
Connecticut River Review: "Maxima Culpa"
Free Lunch: "The Kitchen"
Images: Written and Photographed (Northeast Photography Club): "Alms"
More than Animals: An Anthology Anthology (Redtail Books/Pine Press): "The Migration"
The Ontario Review: "Eyes," "Vector"
Palpable Clock: 25 Years of Mulberry Poets: "The Glass Eye," "The Falcon Club," "The Hug"
Parting Gifts: "Possessed," "The Entrée," "Disrepair"
The Pikestaff Review: "Four Oranges," "The Work"
Poet Lore: "The Twinge"
The Ralph Hughes Scholarship Fund Calendar: "Trumpet" (2010), "Saxology" (2011), "Tone" (2012)
Scanlan's Saloon Poetry Anthology (twin pines press): "Monologue in Scranton's Historic Ironworks," "The Step Falls"
The Sow's Ear Poetry Review: "Bounce"

I would also like to give special thanks to Susan Jaffer, Brian Quinn, and David Elliott for their generous readings of a number of these poems and their invaluable feedback. Special thanks are extended as well to poet Michael Heller, my influential early mentor."

www.ingramcontent.com/pod-product-compliance
Lightning Source LLC
Chambersburg PA
CBHW022013080426
42733CB00007B/592